W9-CNG-285

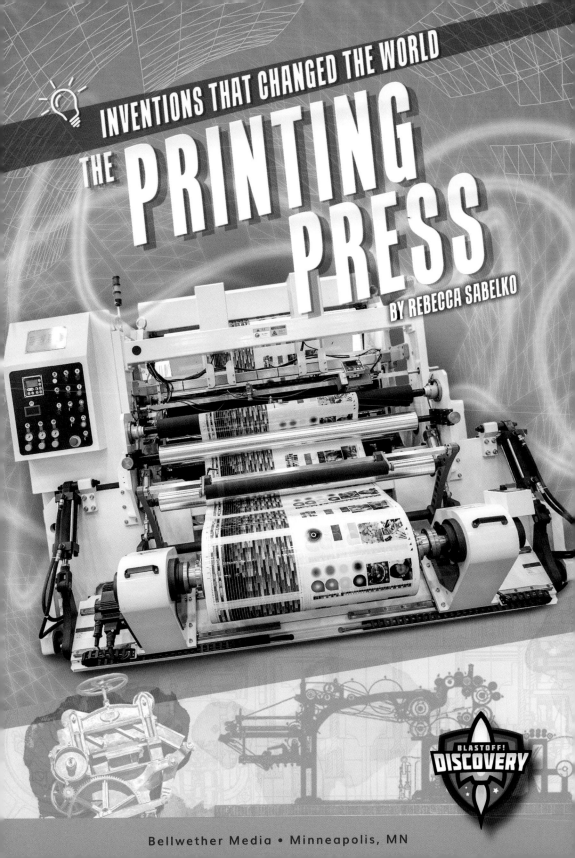

INVENTIONS THAT CHANGED THE WORLD

THE PRINTING PRESS

BY REBECCA SABELKO

BLASTOFF! DISCOVERY

Bellwether Media • Minneapolis, MN

Blastoff! Discovery launches
a new mission: reading to learn.
Filled with facts and features, each
book offers you an exciting new
world to explore!

This edition first published in 2019 by Bellwether Media, Inc.

No part of this publication may be reproduced in whole or in
part without written permission of the publisher.
For information regarding permission, write to Bellwether
Media, Inc., Attention: Permissions Department,
6012 Blue Circle Dr., Minnetonka, MN 55343.

Library of Congress Cataloging-in-Publication Data

Names: Sabelko, Rebecca, author.
Title: The Printing Press / by Rebecca Sabelko.
Description: Minneapolis, MN : Bellwether Media, Inc., 2019.
  | Series: Blastoff! Discovery. Inventions that Changed the
  World | Includes bibliographical references and index. |
  Audience: Ages 7-13.
Identifiers: LCCN 2018040243 (print) | LCCN
  2018041607 (ebook) | ISBN 9781681037042 (ebook)
  | ISBN 9781626179707 (hardcover : alk. paper) | ISBN
  9781618915139 (pbk. : alk. paper)
Subjects: LCSH: Printing presses–History–Juvenile literature.
Classification: LCC Z124 (ebook) | LCC Z124 .S234 2019
  (print) | DDC 681/.6209–dc23
LC record available at https://lccn.loc.gov/2018040243

Text copyright © 2019 by Bellwether Media, Inc. BLASTOFF!
DISCOVERY and associated logos are trademarks
and/or registered trademarks of Bellwether Media, Inc.
SCHOLASTIC, CHILDREN'S PRESS, and associated logos are
trademarks and/or registered trademarks of Scholastic Inc.,
557 Broadway, New York, NY 10012.

Editor: Betsy Rathburn   Designer: Josh Brink

Printed in the United States of America, North Mankato, MN

TABLE OF CONTENTS

A BOOK OF MEMORIES

The yearbook club has worked hard to make this year's yearbook the best their middle school has ever seen! They have spent hours printing out layouts to review. Each colored printout gives them an idea of what the yearbook will look like.

The deadline is only a few days away. Some club members work quickly to review class portraits. Others make sure photos from every sport, dance, and activity are included. Soon, they send their work to the printer!

Workers at the printing company review each page before creating **plates**. Each page gets its own plate. The plates are covered with ink. Then, the images and words are transferred onto paper.

Soon, the books are delivered. The club members admire their work as they turn each bright and colorful page. The yearbooks are soon passed out, and students write notes on the back pages. They laugh over their favorite memories. Thanks to the printing press, the students will remember all the year's special moments forever!

THE STAMPS OF TIME

Humans have recorded ideas for thousands of years! The oldest records of printing are **negative stencil** handprints on cave walls. Later, **cylinder seals** were used to print on clay. Around the year 1000, Chinese printers created woodblock printing. They carved words onto wood. Then, they covered the words in ink and pressed the wood onto paper or cloth.

negative stencil handprints, Cave of the Hands, Argentina

Bi Sheng

Around 1040, Chinese inventor Bi Sheng improved woodblock printing with **movable type**. This method was similar to woodblock printing. But instead of carving into a large block, individual characters were made. They could be arranged and rearranged to make new sentences!

In 1444, printing changed forever. A man named Johannes Gutenberg invented the printing press. This machine made printing with movable type easier than ever. Gutenberg's printing press was much faster than previous printing methods. It could print 250 pages per hour!

Because of the new speed, entire books could be printed in less time. This made owning books less expensive. More people had access to the information they held. This led to major advancements in science, medicine, and technology!

JOHANNES GUTENBERG

Born: 1394 in Mainz, Germany

Background: Inventor who studied metalwork early in life, later using his knowledge to improve movable type printing presses

Year Invented: around 1444

Idea Development: Gutenberg developed his ideas using money he received from a businessman named Johann Fust. After a disagreement between the two men, little of Gutenberg's process was recorded.

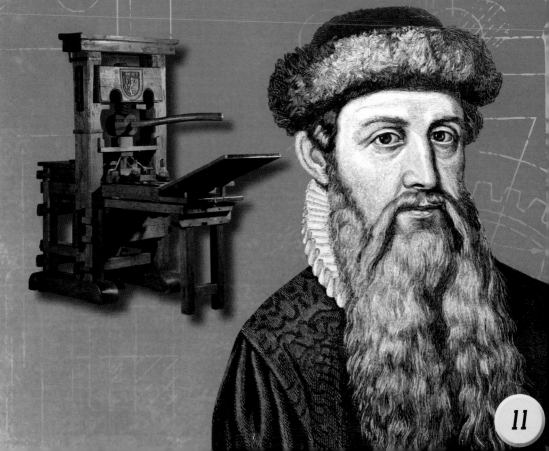

POWERING THE PRINTING PRESS

Gutenberg's printing press meant people no longer had to press letters onto paper themselves. Instead, a machine did it for them. An operator turned a lever to press a large block of movable type onto paper. It was like a big stamp!

Versions of Gutenberg's press were used for hundreds of years. In the 1800s, steam-powered presses made printing even easier. They no longer relied on a human to pull the lever. They could print pages even faster!

lever

stamp

DID YOU KNOW?

The Bible was the first book printed using Gutenberg's press. It was more than 1,200 pages long. Today, Gutenberg Bibles are worth millions of dollars!

By the late 1800s, the **rotary press** was popular. Paper was pressed between two large cylinder rollers. A large metal plate covered the top roller. The plate was **etched** with words and images. Then, it was inked and rolled onto the paper.

In 1875, Robert Barclay used the rotary press to create **offset printing**. A roller beneath the plate roller was covered in a cardboard blanket. This made it easier to print on metal surfaces. By 1903, Ira Washington Rubel improved offset printing. He used a rubber blanket instead of cardboard. This discovery made it easier to print on paper!

rotary press

OFFSET PRINTING PRESS

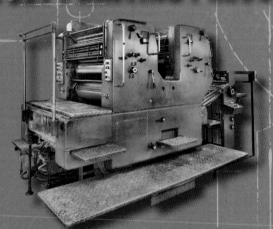

Inventor's Name: Robert Barclay

Year of Release: 1875

Uses: The offset press is a type of rotary press. It uses a series of rollers to print images and words onto books, newspapers, and magazines. Offset presses are usually used only for large printing jobs.

DID YOU KNOW?

Between 600,000 and 1,000,000 books are published in the United States each year. Each of those is printed hundreds of times!

Offset printing is still used today! The process begins with images created on computers. These images are turned into **negatives**. The negative images are transferred to printing plates.

The plates are rolled in water and ink. The area of the plates with images collects ink. The water keeps the ink off the areas without images. Once the plates are rolled, the images are transferred onto a roller covered with a rubber blanket. Large rolls of paper speed through rollers that transfer the images from the rubber sheets onto the paper.

negative images on a printing plate

OFFSET PRINTING PRESS

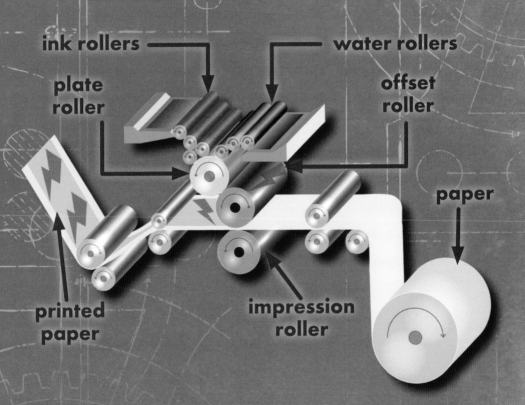

ink rollers

water rollers

plate roller

offset roller

paper

printed paper

impression roller

1. Etched plate roller is coated with water and ink.
2. Plate roller prints design onto offset roller.
3. Paper is fed between offset roller and impression roller. Offset roller prints design on paper.

Offset printing is still the best way to print things like newspapers, magazines, and many copies of books. But it is not the best way to print smaller quantities. Creating the metal plates and rubber blankets can cost hundreds of dollars.

DID YOU KNOW?

Many modern offset presses can fit 8 pages on one press sheet. A press can run 15,000 sheets per hour. This means up to 120,000 pages can be printed per hour!

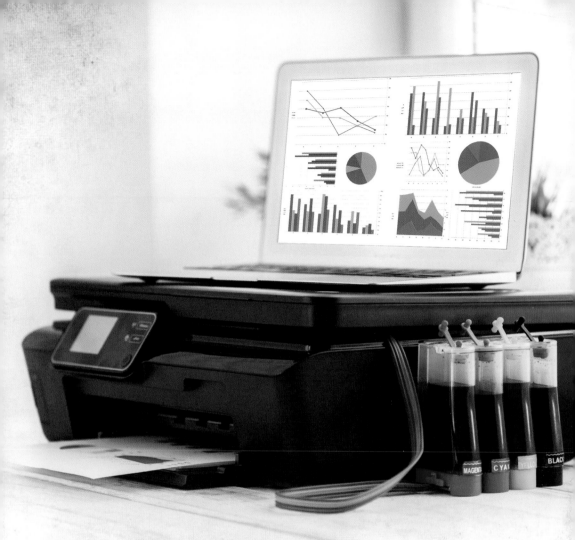

inkjet printer

As technology grows, printing in smaller quantities continues to get cheaper. Today's inkjet and laser printers make personal printing quick and easy. People can print small amounts of documents and photos from computers, flash drives, and even smartphones!

THE GROWTH OF INFORMATION

The invention of the printing press still helps people in the same ways it did hundreds of years ago. One of its biggest impacts is making information available to more people. Today, books are **mass-produced**. This makes them cheaper and more accessible.

Newspapers and magazines bring people information, too. Thousands are printed daily at prices that many people can afford. This high-speed and low-cost printing helps people stay informed!

Printed text and images are seen in so many more places than books and newspapers. Today, print is found on food wrappers, billboards, clothing, and many other items. **Advertisers** use print to get their products and ideas to as many people as possible!

Print helps people stay safe. Traffic signs give drivers directions and rules. Medication and product labels tell people the safe way to use things. The printing press provides information to people every day!

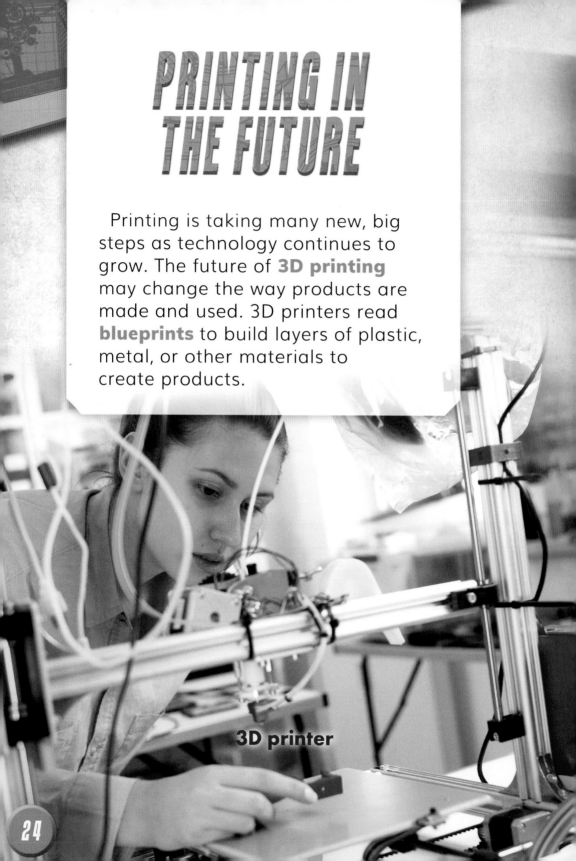

PRINTING IN THE FUTURE

Printing is taking many new, big steps as technology continues to grow. The future of **3D printing** may change the way products are made and used. 3D printers read **blueprints** to build layers of plastic, metal, or other materials to create products.

3D printer

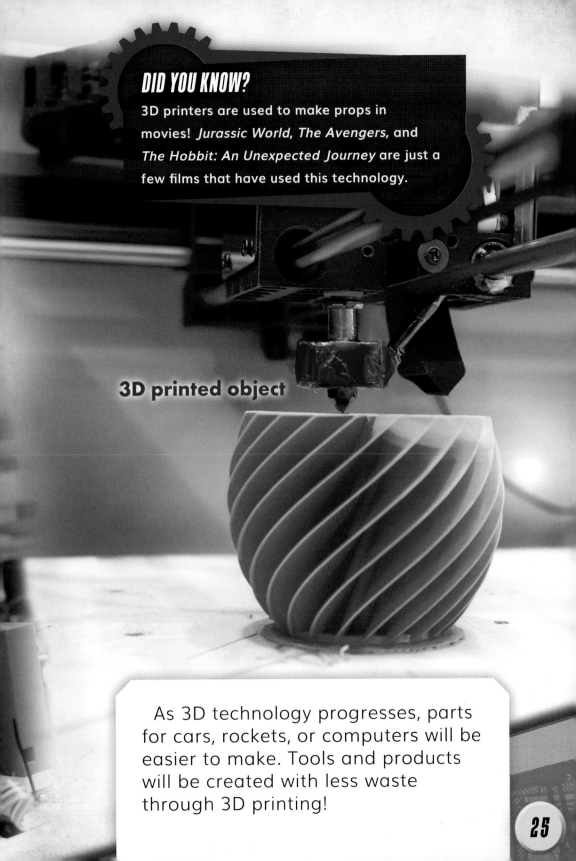

DID YOU KNOW?

3D printers are used to make props in movies! *Jurassic World*, *The Avengers*, and *The Hobbit: An Unexpected Journey* are just a few films that have used this technology.

3D printed object

As 3D technology progresses, parts for cars, rockets, or computers will be easier to make. Tools and products will be created with less waste through 3D printing!

Future printing may take new forms. Scientists may develop invisible printing for increased security. **Conductive inks** are inks that conduct electricity. They are used in many electronic devices. For example, one company found a way to use conductive ink to power **GPS** devices for soldiers!

conductive ink

food-safe ink

Printing may become more Earth-friendly, too. Vegetable-based inks and printer **cartridge** recycling programs would create less waste. Food-safe inks may make food and drink packaging safer. There are many ways print could be used that are still unknown. The future of printing is not yet written!

PRINTING PRESS TIMELINE

3000 BCE
Mesopotamians use round cylinder seals to push images into clay

1444
Johannes Gutenberg's printing press is introduced to the public

1040 CE
Bi Sheng invents the first moveable type out of clay

1812
The steam-powered press is created by Friedrich Koenig and Andreas Friedrich Bauer

1875

Robert Barclay invents offset printing

1969

Xerox invents the first laser printer

1984

3D printing is developed

2019-

Future developments

2012

A team at the University of Illinois create a pen with conductive ink

1843

Richard M. Hoe invents the rotary press

2003

Hewlett Packard launches the first wi-fi printer

GLOSSARY

3D printing—the creation of solid objects by layering material based on directions programmed on a computer

advertisers—companies that make the public aware of something that is being sold

blueprints—detailed plans of how to do something

cartridge—a container that holds ink and is placed into a printer

conductive inks—inks that have the ability to move electricity from one place to another

cylinder seals—small cylinders marked with designs that are rolled onto a soft surface

etched—carved

GPS—global positioning system; GPS is a system that uses satellites to show an object's location.

mass-produced—made in very large quantities

movable type—a system of printing that uses movable letters to print on paper, fabric, or other materials

negative stencil—an image of an object created by coloring in the area around it

negatives—images used for printing photos; negatives reverse the dark and light areas of a subject.

offset printing—a printing process in which inked impressions are first made on a rubber blanket and then transferred to the paper being printed

plates—printing tools that transfer designs onto materials

rotary press—a type of printing press that turns around a central point

TO LEARN MORE

AT THE LIBRARY

Kenney, Karen Latchana. *Cutting-edge 3D Printing*. Minneapolis, Minn.: Lerner Publications, 2019.

Spilsbury, Louise. *Johannes Gutenberg and the Printing Press*. New York, N.Y.: Rosen Publishing Group, Inc., 2016.

Yomtov, Nel. *How the Printing Press Changed History*. Minneapolis, Minn.: Abdo Publishing, 2016.

ON THE WEB

FACTSURFER

Factsurfer.com gives you a safe, fun way to find more information.

1. Go to www.factsurfer.com.

2. Enter "printing press" into the search box.

3. Click the "Surf" button and select your book cover to see a list of related web sites.

INDEX